Hail,
O bright Mother
of the dawning Light!

Theodore of Ancyra

MYSTERIES OF CHRIST

Meditations on the Mysteries of the Rosary

with

St John Paul II

Joyful Mysteries

Mysteries of Light

Sorrowful Mysteries

Glorious Mysteries

The Rosary of the Virgin Mary

SELECTED THOUGHTS FROM

THE APOSTOLIC LETTER BY JOHN PAUL II

The Rosary, though clearly Marian in character, is at heart a Christocentric prayer. In the sobriety of its elements, it has all the *depth of the Gospel message in its entirety*, of which it can be said to be a compendium. It is an echo of the prayer of Mary, her perennial *Magnificat* for the work of the redemptive Incarnation which began in her virginal womb. With the Rosary, the Christian people *sits at the school of Mary* and is led to contemplate the beauty on the face of Christ and to experience the depths of his love. Through the Rosary the faithful receive abundant grace, as though from the very hands of the Mother of the Redeemer…

The Rosary, precisely because it starts with Mary's own experience, is *an exquisitely contemplative prayer.* Without this contemplative dimension, it would lose its meaning… By its nature the recitation of the Rosary calls for a quiet rhythm and a lingering pace, helping the individual to meditate on the mysteries of the Lord's life as seen through the eyes of her who was closest to the Lord…

The Rosary is both *meditation and supplication*. Insistent prayer to the Mother of God is based on confidence that her maternal intercession can obtain all things from the heart of her Son…

The Rosary is by its nature a prayer for peace, since it consists in the contemplation of Christ, the Prince of Peace, the one who is "our peace" *(Eph 2:14)*. Anyone who assimilates the mystery of Christ – and this is clearly the goal of the Rosary – learns the secret of peace and makes it his life's project. Moreover, by virtue of its meditative character, with the tranquil succession of *Hail Marys*, the Rosary has a peaceful effect on those who pray it, disposing them to receive and experience in their innermost depths, and to spread around them, that true peace which is the special gift of the Risen Lord.

We warmly recommend the reading of the entire apostolic letter of John Paul II – "The Rosary of the Virgin Mary", as a source for meditation and a rediscovery of the prayer of the Rosary.

The Rosary Prayer

With his apostolic letter – The Rosary of the Virgin Mary *– John Paul II gives to the whole Church his deep insight on the prayer of the Rosary and introduces a new set of 5 mysteries – The "Mysteries of Light" – to be added to the traditional pattern of the15 mysteries of the Rosary.*

This publication includes a selection of thoughts by John Paul II collected from the whole apostolic letter and gathered under the appropriate heading of each mystery.

The pattern suggested by John Paul II indicates also the distribution of the mysteries during the week, as follows:

The Joyful Mysteries	*Monday and Saturday*
The Mysteries of Light	*Thursday*
The Sorrowful Mysteries	*Tuesday and Friday*
The Glorious Mysteries	*Wednesday and Sunday*

How to Pray the Rosary

John Paul II gives us guidelines on how to pray the Rosary:

1. The announcement of the mystery *with the proclamation of a Biblical passage.*
2. Silence. *Listening and meditating are nourished by silence.*
3. The "Our Father". *In each of his mysteries, Jesus always leads us to the Father.*
4. The ten "Hail Marys". *The repetition of the Hail Mary in the Rosary gives us a share in God's own wonder and pleasure.*
5. The Glory be. *The "Gloria", the high-point of contemplation, has to be given due prominence in the Rosary.*

The Mysteries of the Rosary

Ο ΕΥΑΓΓΕΛΙΣΜΟΣ
διὰ χειρὸς

The Joyful Mysteries

The "joyful mysteries" are marked by

the joy radiating from

the event of the Incarnation.

This is clear from the very first mystery,

the Annunciation,

where Gabriel's greeting to the Virgin of Nazareth

is linked to an invitation to messianic joy:

"Rejoice, Mary".

Ο ΕΥΑΓΓΕΛΙΣΜΟΣ
διὰ χειρὸς
ένης Πρωτοπαπαδάκη
παπακωνσταντίνου 1972

The Annunciation

The angel Gabriel was sent from God to a city of Galilee called Nazareth, to a virgin betrothed to a man whose name was Joseph. The angel said to Mary, "Rejoice you who enjoy God's favour! The Lord is with you. You are to conceive in your womb and bear a son, and you must name him Jesus." Mary said, "I am the handmaid of the Lord."

Lk 1: 26-29, 38

Gabriel's greeting to the Virgin of Nazareth is linked to an invitation to messianic joy: "Rejoice, Mary". The whole of salvation history, in some sense the entire history of the world, has led up to this greeting. If it is the Father's plan to unite all things in Christ, then the whole of the universe is in some way touched by the divine favour with which the Father looks upon Mary and makes her the Mother of his Son. The whole of humanity, in turn, is embraced by the *fiat* with which she readily agrees to the will of God.

RELATED BIBLICAL PASSAGES

Is 7:10-14; 8:10; Mt 1: 18-25; **Lk 1:26-38***; cf Eph 1:1-10; Hb 10:4-10*

διὰ χειρὸς

The Visitation

Mary entered the house of Zechariah and greeted Elizabeth. When Elizabeth heard Mary's greeting, the baby leapt in her womb. She was filled with the Holy Spirit, and giving a loud cry, said, "You are most blessed among women and blessed is the fruit of your womb!"

Lk 1:40-42

Exultation is the keynote of the encounter with Elizabeth, where the sound of Mary's voice and the presence of Christ in her womb cause John "to leap for joy"…

By making our own the words of the Angel Gabriel and Saint Elizabeth contained in the Hail Mary, we find ourselves constantly drawn to seek out afresh in Mary, in her arms and in her heart, the "blessed fruit of her womb".

RELATED BIBLICAL PASSAGES

1 Sam 2:1-10; Is 12:2-6; Zeph 3:14-18; **Lk 1: 39-45**

ΔΟΞΑ ΕΝ ΥΨΙΣΤΟΙΣ ΘΕΩ
ΕΠΙ ΓΗΣ ΕΙΡΗΝΗ
ΕΝ ΑΝΘΡΩΠΟΙ ΕΥΔΟΚΙΑ

The Birth of Jesus

They were in Bethlehem when the time came for Mary to have her child, and she gave birth to a son, her firstborn. She wrapped him in swaddling clothes and laid him in a manger.

Lk 2: 6-7

Gladness also fills the scene in Bethlehem, when the birth of the divine Child, the Saviour of the world, is announced by the song of the angels and proclaimed to the shepherds as "news of great joy"... The contemplation of Christ has an *incomparable model* in Mary. In a unique way the face of the Son belongs to Mary. It was in her womb that Christ was formed, receiving from her a human resemblance which points to an even greater spiritual closeness... When at last she gave birth to him in Bethlehem, her eyes were able to gaze tenderly on the face of her Son, as she "wrapped him in swaddling clothes, and laid him in a manger".

RELATED BIBLICAL PASSAGES

Ps 89 (88). 95 (94). 96 (95). 97 (96); Is 9: 1-7. 52: 7-10. 62: 1-5. 11-12; Mt 2:1-12; **Lk 2:1-20**; *Jn 1:1-5; Gal 4:4-7; Tit 3:4-7; Heb 1:1-6*

Η ΥΠΑ
ΠΑΝΤΗ

The Presentation

When the day came for the purification according to the Law of Moses, Mary and Joseph brought the baby Jesus up to Jerusalem to present him to the Lord. Simeon blessed them and said to Mary, "He shall stand as a sign of contradiction, while a sword will pierce your own soul."

cf Lk 2:22, 34, 35

The Presentation in the Temple not only expresses the joy of the Child's consecration and the ecstasy of the aged Simeon; it also records the prophecy that Christ will be a "sign of contradiction" for Israel and that a sword will pierce his mother's heart... Mary lived with her eyes fixed on Christ, treasuring his every word: "She kept all these things, pondering them in her heart." The memories of Jesus, impressed upon her heart, were always with her, leading her to reflect on the various moments of her life at her Son's side.

RELATED BIBLICAL PASSAGES

Ps 24 (23); Mal 3:1-4; **Lk 2:22-40***; 18-20; Heb 2:14-18*

The Finding in the Temple

When Jesus was twelve years old, he went up to Jerusalem with his parents, according to the custom for the feast. After the festival was over, Mary and Joseph returned, but the boy Jesus remained in Jerusalem and his parents did not know it. On the third day they found him in the Temple, sitting among the teachers, listening to them and asking questions.

cf Lk 2:42-43, 46

Joy mixed with drama marks the fifth mystery: the finding of the twelve-year-old Jesus in the Temple. Here he appears in his divine wisdom as he listens and raises questions, already in effect one who "teaches". The revelation of his mystery as the Son wholly dedicated to his Father's affairs proclaims the radical nature of the Gospel, in which even the closest of human relationships are challenged by the absolute demands of the Kingdom. Mary and Joseph, fearful and anxious, "did not understand" his words.

RELATED BIBLICAL PASSAGES

Mt 23:1-12; **Lk 2:41-50***; Jn 4:31-34. 7:15-16*

Ἡ ΜΕΤΑ
ΜΟΡΦΩϹ

The Mysteries of Light

Moving on from the infancy

and the hidden life in Nazareth

to the public life of Jesus,

our contemplation brings us

to those mysteries which may be called

in a special way "mysteries of light".

Certainly the whole mystery of Christ

is a mystery of light.

He is the "light of the world".

Η ΒΑ ΠΗCΙC
διὰ χειρὸς
Ἑλένης

The Baptism in the Jordan

Jesus arrived from Galilee and came to John at the Jordan to be baptised by him. As soon as he was baptised, he came up from the water and a voice from heaven was heard, "This is my son, the Beloved; he is my chosen one."
cf Mt 3:13, 16-17

The Baptism in the Jordan is, first of all, a mystery of light. Here, as Christ descends into the waters, the innocent one who became "sin" for our sake, the heavens open wide and the voice of the Father declares him the beloved Son while the Spirit descends on him to invest him with the mission which he is to carry out... Christian spirituality is distinguished by the disciple's commitment to become conformed ever more fully to his Master. The outpouring of the Holy Spirit in Baptism grafts the believer like a branch onto the vine which is Christ and makes him a member of Christ's mystical Body.

RELATED BIBLICAL PASSAGES

Is 40:1-5.9-11; 55:1-11; 42:1-4. 6-7; Ezek 36:25-27; **Mt 3:13-17**; *Mk 1:9-11; Lk 3:15-22; Acts 10:34-38; Rom 8:29; 1Cor 12:12; Tit 2:11-14. 3:4-7; 1 Jn 5:1-9*

Ο ΕΝ
ΚΑΝΑ ΓΑΜΟΣ
ΜΡ ΘΥ
Ο ΩΝ

The Manifestation of Jesus at Cana

There was a wedding at Cana in Galilee and the mother of Jesus was there. Jesus was also invited with his disciples. As they had run out of wine, the mother of Jesus said to him, "They have no wine." Jesus replied, "Woman, your thoughts are not mine! My hour has not yet come." His mother said to the servants, "Do whatever he tells you." cf Jn 2:1-5

The first of the "signs" worked by Jesus – the changing of water into wine at the marriage in Cana – clearly presents Mary in the guise of a teacher, as she urges the servants to do what Jesus commands. At the wedding in Cana the Gospel clearly shows the power of Mary's intercession as she makes known to Jesus the needs of others: "They have no wine"…

Mary's gaze would always be a *penetrating gaze,* one capable of deeply understanding Jesus, even to the point of perceiving his hidden feelings and anticipating his decisions… This school of Mary is all the more effective if we consider that she teaches by obtaining for us in abundance the gifts of the Holy Spirit, even as she offers us the incomparable example of her own "pilgrimage of faith".

RELATED BIBLICAL PASSAGES

Is 25:6-2-1; Mt 12:46-50; **Jn 2:1-12**

ΠΟΡΕΥΘΈΝΤΕϹ ΜΑΘΗΤΕΎϹΑΤΕ
ΠΆΝΤΑ ΤᾺ ἜΘΝΗ

The Proclamation of the Kingdom

After John was arrested, Jesus went into Galilee and began preaching the Good News of God. He said, "The time has come; the kingdom of God is at hand. Repent and believe the Gospel."
Mk 1:14-15

Declared the beloved Son of the Father at the Baptism in the Jordan, Christ is the one who announces the coming of the Kingdom, bears witness to it in his works and proclaims its demands. It is during the years of his public ministry that *the mystery of Christ is most evidently a mystery of light:* "While I am in the world, I am the light of the world..."

Mystery of light is the preaching by which Jesus proclaims the coming of the Kingdom of God, calls to conversion and forgives the sins of all who draw near to him in humble trust: the inauguration of that ministry of mercy which he continues to exercise until the end of the world, particularly through the Sacrament of Reconciliation which he has entrusted to his Church.

RELATED BIBLICAL PASSAGES

Mt 4:12-17; **Mk 1:14-15***; 2:3-13; Lk 4:14-22; 7:47- 48; Jn 9:5. 20:22-23*

Ἡ ΜΕΤΑ
ΜΟΡΦωCIC

The Transfiguration

Jesus took with him Peter and James and John, and led them up a high mountain. There his appearance was changed before their eyes. A cloud formed, covering them in a shadow, and from this cloud came these words, "This is my Son, the Beloved; listen to him." Lk 9:28ff

The mystery of light *par excellence* is the Transfiguration, traditionally believed to have taken place on Mount Tabor. The glory of the Godhead shines forth from the face of Christ as the Father commands the astonished Apostles to "listen to him" and to prepare to experience with him the agony of the Passion, so as to come with him to the joy of the Resurrection and a life transfigured by the Holy Spirit…

The Gospel scene of Christ's transfiguration, in which the three Apostles appear entranced by the beauty of the Redeemer, can be seen as *an icon of Christian contemplation*. To look upon the face of Christ, to recognise its mystery amid the daily events and the sufferings of his human life, and then to grasp the divine splendour definitively revealed in the Risen Lord: this is the task of every follower of Christ and therefore the task of each one of us.

RELATED BIBLICAL PASSAGES

Dan 7:9-10.13-14; Mt 17:1-8; Mk 9:2-8; **Lk 9:28-36**; *Jn 1:29-34; 2 Pet 1:16-19*

Ὁ ΜΥΣΤΙΚΟΣ
ΔΕΙΠΝΟΣ

Institution of the Eucharist

Jesus took his place at table and his apostles with him. Jesus took the bread, he broke it and gave it to them saying, "This is my body which is given for you. Do this in remembrance of me." And he did the same with the cup, saying, "This cup is the new covenant, sealed in my blood which is poured out for you." *cf Lk 22:14, 19-20*

The institution of the Eucharist, in which Christ offers his body and blood as food under the signs of bread and wine, testifies "to the end" his love for humanity, for whose salvation he will offer himself in sacrifice...

In these mysteries... *the presence of Mary remains in the background.* The Gospels make only the briefest reference to her occasional presence at one moment or other during the preaching of Jesus, and they give no indication that she was present at the Last Supper and the institution of the Eucharist. Yet the role she assumed at Cana in some way accompanies Christ throughout his ministry. The revelation made directly by the Father at the Baptism in the Jordan and echoed by John the Baptist is placed upon Mary's lips at Cana, and it becomes the great maternal counsel which Mary addresses to the Church of every age: "Do whatever he tells you."

RELATED BIBLICAL PASSAGES

Deut 8:2-3.14-16; Mt 26:26-29; Mk 14:22-25; **Lk 22:15-20***;*
Jn 2:5.12; 6:51-58; 13:1-16; 1Cor 10:16-17. 11:23-26; Heb 9:11-15

IC XC
διὰ χειρ
Ἑλένης Πρωτοπα

The Sorrowful Mysteries

The Gospels give great prominence

to the sorrowful mysteries of Christ…

The Rosary selects

certain moments from the Passion,

inviting the faithful

to contemplate them

in their hearts and to relive them.

Ἡ ΠΡΟΣΕΥΧῊ ἘΝ ΤΩ͂Ι ΚΉΠΩΙ ΤΗ͂Σ ΓΕΘΣΗΜΑΝΗ͂

The Agony in the Garden

They came to a place which was called Gethsemane and Jesus said to his disciples, "Sit here while I pray." Then he went a little further on and fell to the ground, praying that if possible this hour might pass him by. Jesus said, "Abba, all things are possible for you; take this cup away from me. Yet not what I want but what you want."

cf Mk 14:32, 35-36

The sequence of meditations begins with Gethsemane, where Christ experiences a moment of great anguish before the will of the Father, against which the weakness of the flesh would be tempted to rebel. There Jesus encounters all the temptations and confronts all the sins of humanity, in order to say to the Father: "Not my will but yours be done." This "Yes" of Christ reverses the "No" of our first parents in the Garden of Eden.

RELATED BIBLICAL PASSAGES

Mt 26:36-46; **Mk 14:32-42**; *Lk 22:39-46; Jn 18:1-11; Rom 8:26-27*

Ο ΧΡΙΣΤΟΣ ΚΡΙΝΟΜΕΝΟΣ ΥΠΟ ΤΟΥ ΠΙΛΑΤΟΥ
διὰ χειρὸς

The Scourging at the Pillar

As Pilate wanted to please the people, he freed Barabbas, and after the scourging of Jesus, had him handed over to be crucified.

Mt 27:26

The cost of Jesus' faithfulness to the Father's will is made clear in the following mysteries… From the beginning Christian piety, especially during the Lenten devotion of the *Way of the Cross*, has focused on the individual moments of the Passion, realising that here is found *the culmination of the revelation of God's love* and the source of our salvation.

RELATED BIBLICAL PASSAGES

Is 52:13-15. 53:1-9; **Mt 27:11-26***; Mk 15:1-15; 1Pet 2:21-24; 1 Jn 4:7-10*

Ὁ ἘΜΠΑΙΓΜΌΣ
ΙC ΧC
διὰ χειρὸς
Πρωτοπαπαδάκη

The Crowning with Thorns

They stripped Jesus and dressed him in a purple cloak. Then twisting a crown of thorns, they forced it onto his head, and placed a reed in his right hand. They knelt before Jesus and mocked him, saying, "Long life to the King of the Jews!"

Mt 27:28-30

With his scourging, his crowning with thorns, his carrying the Cross and his death on the Cross, the Lord is cast into the most abject suffering: *Ecce homo!*

This abject suffering reveals not only the love of God but also the meaning of man himself.

RELATED BIBLICAL PASSAGES

Is 50:4-9; **Mt 27:27-31***; Mk 15:16-20; Lk 22:63-65*

Ὁ ΧΡΙϹΤῸϹ ἙΛΚΌΜΕΝΟϹ ἘΠῚ ϹΤΑΥΡΟΥ͂
Ὁ ὬΝ

The Carrying of the Cross

They took charge of Jesus. Bearing his own cross, he went out of the city to what is called the Place of the Skull, in Hebrew: Golgotha.

Jn 19:17

Ecce homo: the meaning, origin and fulfilment of man is to be found in Christ, the God who humbles himself out of love "even unto death, death on a cross"... How could one contemplate Christ carrying the Cross and Christ Crucified, without feeling the need to act as a Simon of Cyrene for our brothers and sisters weighed down by grief or crushed by despair?

RELATED BIBLICAL PASSAGES

Mt 11:28-30; 27:32-34; Mk 15:21-22; **Lk 23:26-32**; *Jn 19:17*

IC XC

The Crucifixion

Near the cross of Jesus stood his mother, his mother's sister Mary and Mary of Magdala. When Jesus saw his mother and the disciple whom he loved, he said to the mother, "Woman, this is your son." Then he said to the disciple, "This is your mother."

Jn 19:25-27

The sorrowful mysteries help the believer to relive the death of Jesus, to stand at the foot of the Cross beside Mary, to enter with her into the depths of God's love for us and to experience all its life-giving power…

Mary's gaze, ever filled with adoration and wonder, would never leave him… At times it would be a look of sorrow, especially beneath the Cross, where her vision would still be that of a mother giving birth, for Mary not only shared the passion and death of her Son, she also received the new son given to her in the beloved disciple.

RELATED BIBLICAL PASSAGES

Mt 27:35-56; Mk 15:23-39; Lk 23:44-46; **Jn** *12:23-32.* **19:17-30**; *Phil 2:6-11*

Ἡ ἈΝΑϹΤΑϹΙϹ

The Glorious Mysteries

The Rosary has always

expressed this knowledge

born of faith

and invited the believer

to pass beyond

the darkness of the Passion

in order to gaze upon Christ's glory

in the Resurrection and Ascension.

῾Η ᾿ΑΝΆϹΤΑϹΙϹ

The Resurrection

On the first day of the week, at dawn, the women went to the tomb with the perfumes and ointments they had prepared. Two men in dazzling garments appeared beside them. In fright the women bowed to the ground. But the men said, "Why do you look for the living among the dead? You won't find him here. He is risen."

cf Lk 24:1, 4-6

The contemplation of Christ's face cannot stop at the image of the Crucified One. "He is the Risen One!" Contemplating the Risen One, Christians *rediscover the reasons for their own faith* and relive the joy not only of those to whom Christ appeared – the Apostles, Mary Magdalene and the disciples on the road to Emmaus – but also *the joy of Mary*, who must have had an equally intense experience of the new life of her glorified Son.

RELATED BIBLICAL PASSAGES

Mt 28:1-10; Mk 16:1-8; **Lk 24:1-12***; Jn 20:1-10. 11-18; 1 Cor 15:11-19; Col 3:1-4*

The Ascension

Jesus was taken up before the disciples' eyes and a cloud hid him from their sight. Suddenly two men dressed in white stood beside them and said, "Men of Galilee why do you stand here looking up at the sky"? This Jesus, who has been taken from you into heaven, will return in the same way as you have seen him go there."

cf Acts 1:9-11

In the Ascension, Christ was raised in glory to the right hand of the Father, while Mary herself would be raised to that same glory in the Assumption, enjoying beforehand, by a unique privilege, the destiny reserved for all the just at the resurrection of the dead.

RELATED BIBLICAL PASSAGES

Mt 28:16-20; Mk 16:14-20; Lk 24:50-53; **Acts 1:1-11***; Eph 1:17-23*

Ἡ ΠΕΝΤΗ-
-ΚΟΣΤΉ

The Descent of the Holy Spirit

When Pentecost day came, the apostles were all together in one place. Suddenly out of the sky came a sound like a strong rushing wind. There appeared tongues as if of fire which parted and came to rest upon each one of them. All were filled with the Holy Spirit and began to speak other languages, as the Spirit enabled them to speak.

cf Acts 2:1-4

The third glorious mystery, Pentecost, reveals the face of the Church as a family gathered together with Mary, enlivened by the powerful outpouring of the Spirit and ready for the mission of evangelization… Mary who is both the Mother of Christ and a member of the Church, indeed her "pre-eminent and altogether singular member", is at the same time the "Mother of the Church". As such, she continually brings to birth children for the mystical Body of her Son. She does so through her intercession, imploring upon them the inexhaustible outpouring of the Spirit.

RELATED BIBLICAL PASSAGES

Jn 15:26-27. 16:12-15; 20:19-23; **Acts** *1:12-14;* **2:1-11**. *36- 41; Gal 5:16-25*

Ἡ ΜΕΤΑCΤΑCΙC
ΤΗC ΘΕΟΤΚΥ
ΜΡ ΘΥ
διά χειρός

The Assumption of Mary

Jesus said to his disciples, "After I have gone and prepared a place for you, I shall come again and take you to me, so that where I am, you also may be."

Jn 14:3

The glorious mysteries lead the faithful to *greater hope for the eschatological goal* towards which they journey as members of the pilgrim People of God in history. This can only impel them to bear courageous witness to that "good news" which gives meaning to their entire existence.

RELATED BIBLICAL PASSAGES

Sg 2:10, 11; Is 61:10; Mt 25:1-13; **Jn 14:1-3***; 1 Cor 15:51-52; Lk 1:46-55*

The Crowning of Mary

A great sign appeared in heaven: a woman, clothed with the sun, with the moon under her feet and a crown of twelve stars on her head.

Rev 12:1

Crowned in glory – as she appears in the last glorious mystery – Mary shines forth as Queen of the Angels and Saints, the anticipation and the supreme realisation of the eschatological state of the Church…

How could one possibly gaze upon the glory of the Risen Christ or of Mary Queen of Heaven, without yearning to make this world more beautiful, more just, more closely conformed to God's plan? Contemplating Christ and his Blessed Mother in glory, believers see the goal towards which each of us is called, if we allow ourselves to be healed and transformed by the Holy Spirit.

RELATED BIBLICAL PASSAGES

Ps 87 (86):1-3, 5-7; Ps 45 (44) 10-12, 16; Is 61:10-11; Rev 12:1-19

Table of Plates

All the works by Helen Protopapadakis – Papaconstantinou (H.P.P.) take their inspiration from original ancient icons.

First edition published in the United Kingdom as *Mysteries of Light*, 2003
This edition published in the United Kingdom in 2014
Pauline Books & Media
Slough, SL3 6BS, England

From the Apostolic Letter of John Paul II ***Rosarium Virginis Mariae***

Scripture texts from the ***Christian Community Bible***
© 1999 Bernardo Hurault, Claretion Publication

Icon reproductions Helen Protopapadakis-Papaconstantinou
Edited by Rina Risitano, fsp
Graphic design by Pauline Books & Media UK

ISBN 978-1-904785-68-2

Pauline
BOOKS & MEDIA

Middle Green, Slough SL3 6BS – UK
+44 (0) 1753 577629
www.pauline-uk.org
marketing@pauline-uk.org

Pauline Books & Media is an expression of the ministry of the Daughters of St Paul, an international Catholic community of religious women, dedicated to spreading the Good News of Jesus Christ. In imitation of the Apostle Paul, who used every means to proclaim Christ, the sisters work with modern media and technology for evangelisation.